What Is the Story of Cinderella?

by Dana Meachen Rau

illustrated by David Malan

Penguin Workshop

To my own smart, courageous,
and kind princess—DMR

For my princess, Alice—DM

PENGUIN WORKSHOP
An imprint of Penguin Random House LLC
1745 Broadway, New York, New York 10019

First published in the United States of America by Penguin Workshop,
an imprint of Penguin Random House LLC, 2025

Copyright © 2025 by Penguin Random House LLC

Penguin Random House values and supports copyright. Copyright fuels creativity, encourages diverse voices, promotes free speech, and creates a vibrant culture. Thank you for buying an authorized edition of this book and for complying with copyright laws by not reproducing, scanning, or distributing any part of it in any form without permission. You are supporting writers and allowing Penguin Random House to continue to publish books for every reader. Please note that no part of this book may be used or reproduced in any manner for the purpose of training artificial intelligence technologies or systems.

PENGUIN is a registered trademark and PENGUIN WORKSHOP is a trademark
of Penguin Books Ltd. WHO HQ & Design is a registered trademark
of Penguin Random House LLC.

Visit us online at penguinrandomhouse.com.

Library of Congress Cataloging-in-Publication Data is available.

Printed in the United States of America

ISBN 9780593754283 (paperback)　　　　　10 9 8 7 6 5 4 3 2 1 CJKW
ISBN 9780593754290 (library binding)　　　10 9 8 7 6 5 4 3 2 1 CJKW

The publisher does not have any control over and does not assume any responsibility
for author or third-party websites or their content.

Contents

What Is the Story of Cinderella? 1
The Flying Sandal 6
The Magical Fish 14
The Giving Tree 28
Fairies, Pumpkins, and Glass Shoes 39
A Dark Turn 52
Stepping Off the Page 66
A Popular Princess 76
Her Own Hero 88
A Modern Cinderella 96
Bibliography 106

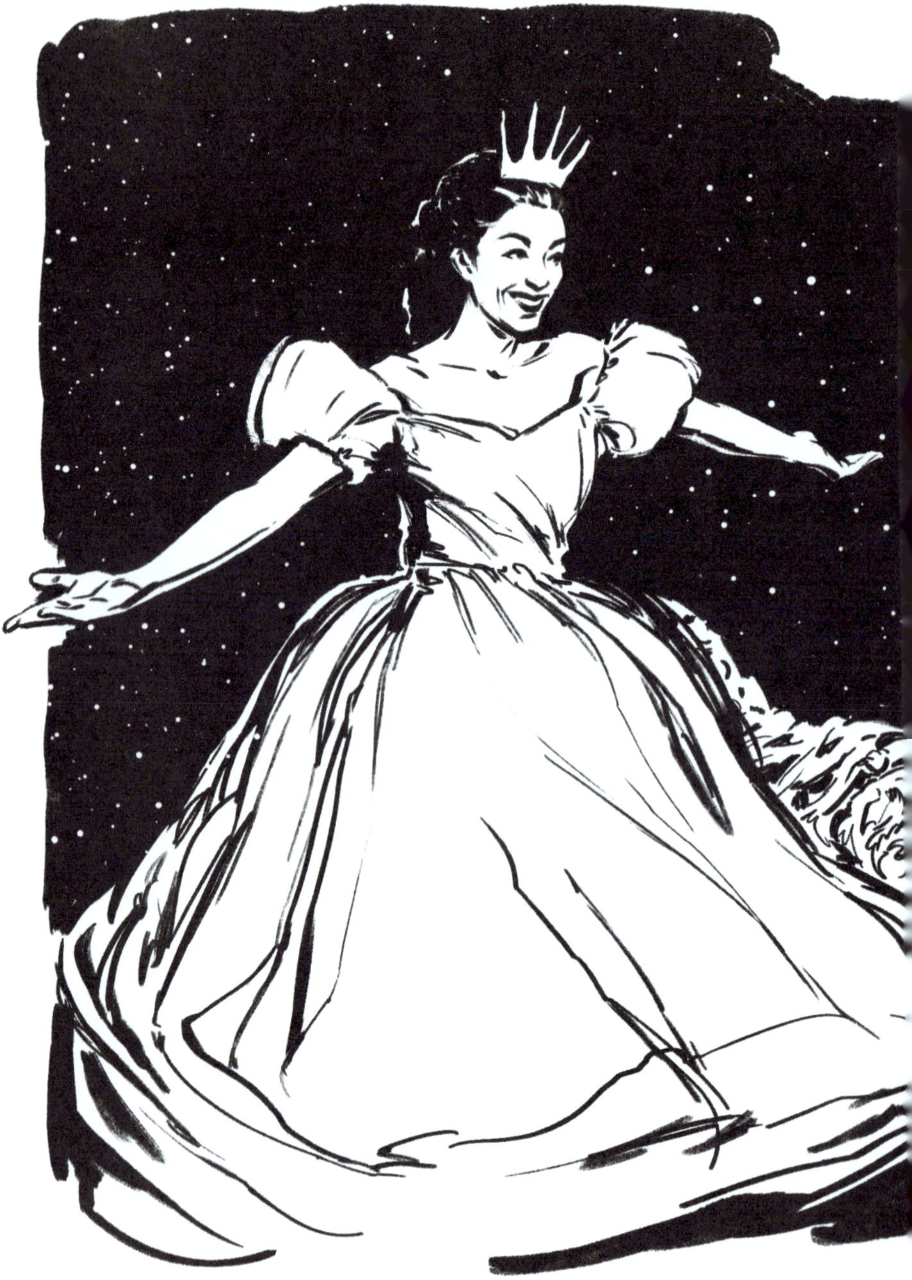

What Is the Story of Cinderella?

Once upon a time, on a stage in New York City in 2014, Cinderella twirled. Her dress turned from rags into a beautiful gown in front of an amazed audience.

The actress Keke Palmer played the popular princess in the Broadway show *Rodgers and Hammerstein's Cinderella*. As a child, she had dreamed of acting, singing, and dancing on Broadway someday. But she never imagined it would happen when she was only twenty-one years old. She had always liked the fairy tale about a hardworking girl who had big dreams. Keke was thrilled to be the title character in a story that proved all things are possible if you believe.

Most everyone has heard of the princess Cinderella. In the popular fairy tale, Cinderella is a poor servant who is treated cruelly by her stepmother and stepsisters. After some magical help, she goes to a royal ball where she and a prince fall in love. When the clock strikes midnight, she rushes away, leaving only a shoe behind. The prince has all the maidens in the kingdom try on the shoe in order to find her. When he does, they marry, and Cinderella becomes a princess.

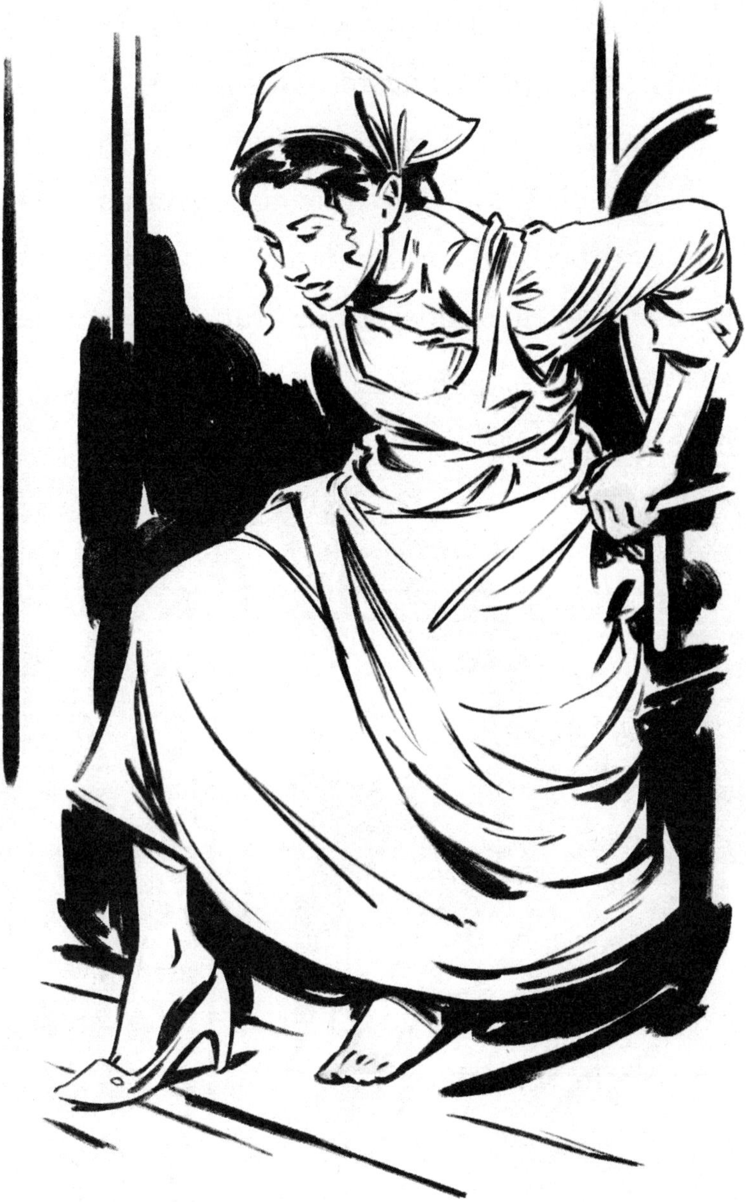

While the character Cinderella is familiar, many people haven't heard of Rhodopis, Ye Xian, Zezolla, Cendrillon, and Aschenputtel. They are all Cinderellas, too! These characters start as poor girls and become royalty by the end. Cinderella as we know her today came from these earlier stories.

Characters in fiction books are imagined by the author. But Cinderella was not created by one author in one story. Cinderella-like characters have appeared in many cultures over thousands of years in hundreds of stories. Most of these tales have a moral, or a lesson the reader learns when they read the story. This is often the same: Cruelty will get you nowhere, and kindness deserves the biggest reward.

Cinderella's story has been retold so many times throughout history because everyone can relate to her. Like Cinderella, everyone feels down at times and hopes for a better life. Everyone wants their wishes to come true.

CHAPTER 1
The Flying Sandal

Storytelling has always been an important part of how people communicate with each other throughout history. Before people even created writing, they drew pictures on cave walls to tell stories. Groups also gathered together and listened to stories being told out loud. These tales had a purpose in a community: They entertained listeners, but they also passed down important history and taught lessons about the world. As cultures created written languages, people started writing down stories.

In those early times, it was not as easy to travel as it is today, which meant the stories stayed within the area where they were first told. But eventually people started to explore. They traded goods and ideas with other cultures. They shared their stories, too. Travelers brought tales home and retold them.

The storyteller sometimes changed parts and added details so that listeners could better understand the story, creating a new version of the original.

The story of Cinderella was first written down about two thousand years ago in ancient Greece. Strabo (say: STRAY-bow) was a geographer, historian, and writer born in 64 BCE. At the time, people didn't know much about how the world looked. So Strabo traveled the lands around the Mediterranean Sea and into northern Africa. He mapped those areas and wrote history and geography books about what he'd discovered.

Strabo

In his book *Geography*, Strabo describes the

sights he saw on a trip to Egypt. A guide took him to see the Pyramids of Giza—three huge stone structures built as tombs for pharaohs, or kings.

Strabo was told that the smallest pyramid honored a woman called Rhodopis (say: RO-dop-is), which means "rosy cheeked." They also told Strabo a story about her.

Rhodopis

Rhodopis, a beautiful but poor woman, was bathing in the Nile River. An eagle swooped down and snatched one of her sandals from the bank.

It flew far away, down the river to the city of Memphis in Egypt where the pharaoh lived.

The pharaoh was leading an outdoor meeting. The eagle dropped the sandal into his lap. Surprised, the pharaoh looked at it closely. He had to know who wore such a beautiful shoe!

He ordered men to search throughout Egypt for the sandal's owner. They found Rhodopis and brought her to the pharaoh. Rhodopis and the pharaoh married, and she became queen.

The Rhodopis story does not have all the details of the Cinderella story we know today. But it contains the most basic parts: A poor girl loses a shoe, and a royal person finds it. A king sends out a search party, and when the girl is found, they marry.

While Rhodopis was a real woman in the sixth century BCE, this story about her is likely not true. But most historians agree that Strabo's early description of Rhodopis is the very first Cinderella story.

Ancient Scrolls

Today, books are filled with printed sheets of paper bound together between covers. But in ancient Greece, reading a story looked very different.

Words were handwritten on papyrus, which was made by pounding together fibers of the papyrus plant to make a paper-like surface. Sheets of papyrus were connected to form one long piece. This piece could be rolled up into a scroll. The text was written in columns so that readers could unroll part of the scroll, read a column, then unroll the next bit, and continue until they reached the end of the whole piece.

CHAPTER 2
The Magical Fish

About nine hundred years after Rhodopis, Chinese writer Duan Chengshi (say: DWAN CHUNG SHHH) wrote another Cinderella-like story. Duan was born to a wealthy family.

Ye Xian

He was supposed to assist his father in government. Instead, he spent his days on hunting trips. And he always brought stories home with him. Around 850 to 860 CE, Duan wrote a book called *Miscellaneous Morsels from Youyang*. It was a collection of tales from an earlier time that he had heard and read. Many of the stories contained magic, including a folktale about a girl named Ye Xian (say: YEH she-ehn).

He wrote that he had heard the story from one of his family's servants who was from the area where this event supposedly took place.

Ye Xian was a smart and talented girl. When her mother died, and then her father, she was left in the care of her stepmother, who also had a daughter. The stepmother worked Ye Xian very hard, making her fetch water and gather firewood in deep and dangerous places.

One day while Ye Xian collected water, she caught a small fish, only about two inches long. It was so beautiful, with golden eyes and red fins, that she wanted to keep it. So she placed it in a bowl of water. The fish grew larger every day.

She had to keep finding bigger and bigger bowls to hold it. Soon it was so big that Ye Xian had to release it in a pond where it would have lots of room to grow.

Ye Xian visited the fish often to feed it leftovers. When she visited, the fish greeted her by poking its head above the water and resting it on the bank. It had grown to more than seven feet long.

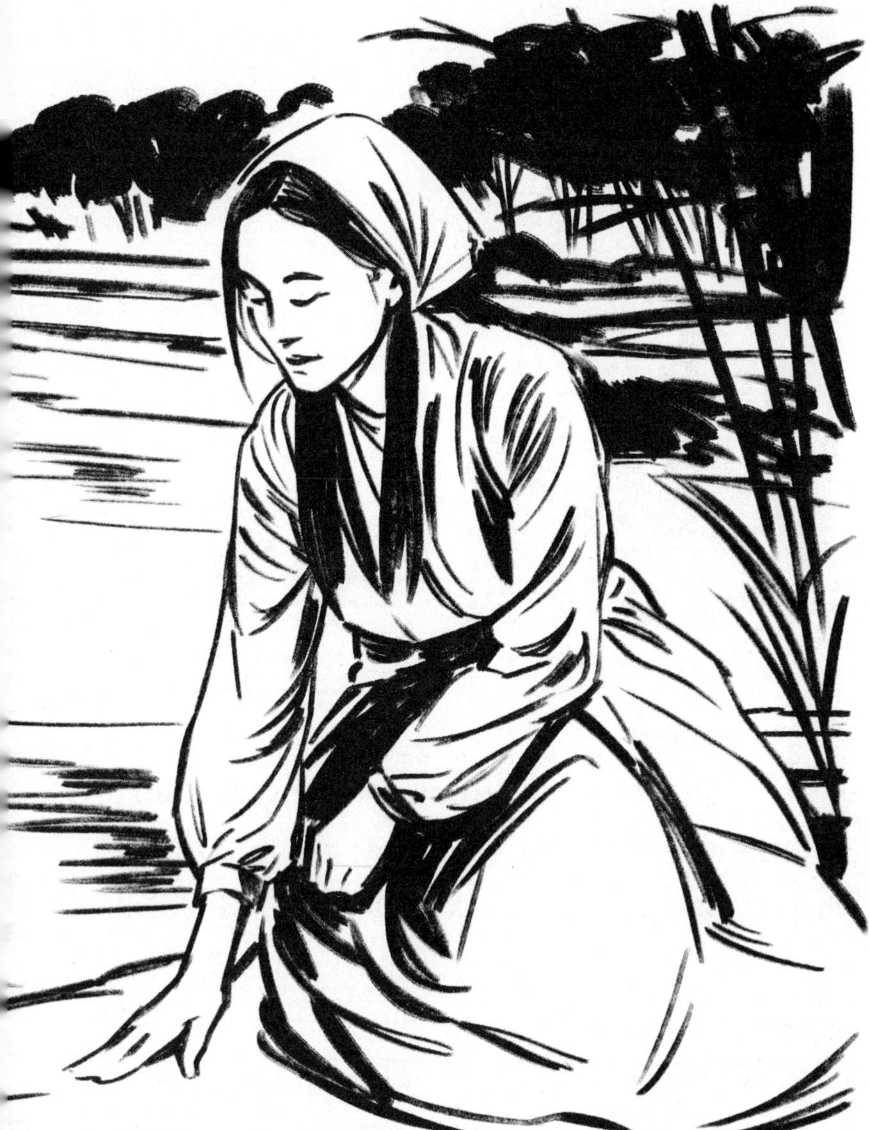

The stepmother had been watching Ye Xian. She noticed that the fish didn't come out for anyone except her stepdaughter. She decided to play a trick. "Haven't you worked hard!" the stepmother said to Ye Xian. She told Ye Xian to take off her own tattered clothes and put on a new dress. Then she sent Ye Xian to get water from a faraway spring. While Ye Xian was gone, the stepmother put on the old clothes and went to the pond. The fish thought Ye Xian had come to visit. When it came to the surface, the stepmother chopped off its head. She cooked it, ate the delicious fish, and hid the bones in the dirt.

The next day, Ye Xian went to the pond and cried that her fish was gone. Suddenly, a man came down from the sky. "Don't howl!" he said. He told her what the stepmother had done. "You go back, take the fish's bones and hide them in your room." He told her to wish on the bones for anything she wanted.

Soon it was festival time. Ye Xian's stepmother and stepsister headed off to celebrate. They left her home to work, but Ye Xian had another plan. She wished for something to wear. Dressed in gold shoes and a cloak made of kingfisher feathers, she headed off to the festival, too.

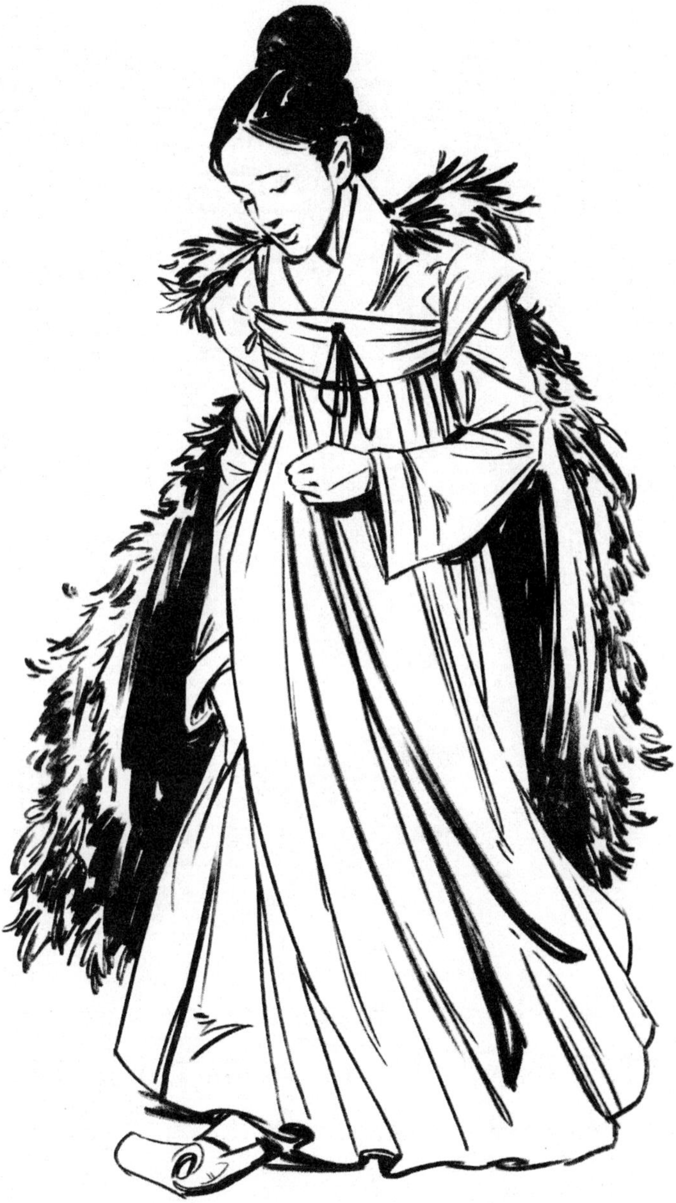

While she was there, her stepsister recognized her. Ye Xian rushed home, leaving a shoe behind by mistake. When the stepmother and stepsister returned, they found Ye Xian asleep, leaning against a tree. They thought she hadn't been at the festival after all.

Meanwhile, someone had taken the shoe to the nearby island kingdom of Tuo Han to sell it. The little, light, delicate shoe ended up in the hands of the king. He was determined to find its owner. He ordered every woman in his kingdom to try it on until he finally found Ye Xian. The shoe fit!

He took her, and the fish bones, back to his country. The stepmother and stepsister were punished for their cruelty and killed with flying stones.

The king married Ye Xian. Then over the next year, he greedily wished on the bones for treasure.

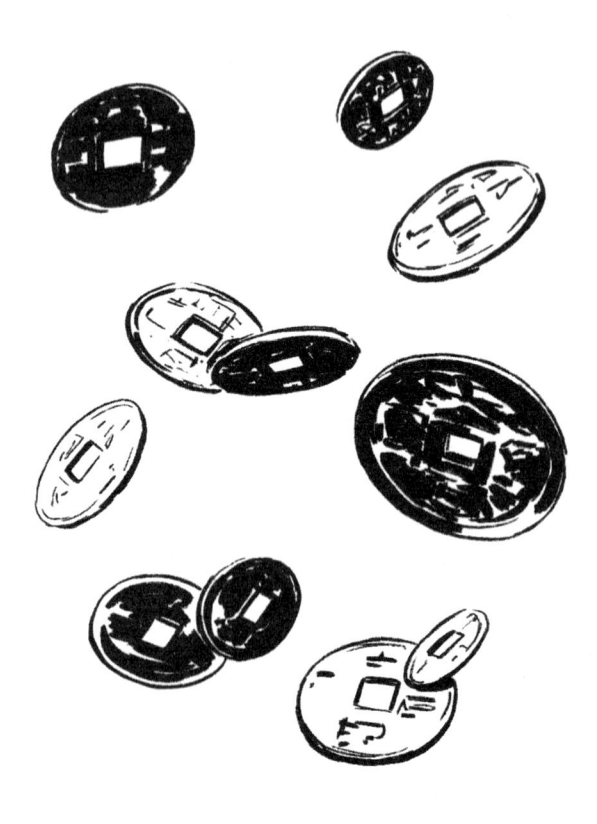

When the bones stopped giving him what he wanted, he buried them. Later, when someone tried to dig them up, the bones had been washed away.

This story adds some details that are very familiar to readers today—a cruel stepmother, magic that grants wishes, and of course, a big party! And like Rhodopis, a poor hardworking girl becomes a queen in the end. But unlike the kings and princes in later stories, this love interest is selfish and unkind.

CHAPTER 3
The Giving Tree

As time went on, travelers shared and traded more goods, ideas, and stories between countries. Folktales with Cinderella characters appeared in many cultures. The next well-known version was written in Naples, Italy, by Giambattista Basile (say: JEE-ahm-bat-tees-tuh bah-SEE-leh). "The Cat Cinderella," or "La Gatta Cenerentola" appears in his fifty-story collection called *Tale of Tales* published in 1634. Basile spent lots of time visiting the courts of Italian princes. Royal courts were often busy places with people from all

Giambattista Basile

over the world. Basile wrote down folktales he heard from them, adding Italian details.

His main character, Zezolla, is already a princess at the beginning of her story. Her mother had died, so the girl was taught by her governess, Carmosina. When her father remarried, the new stepmother was cruel. Zezolla complained to her governess. Carmosina had a plan. She told Zezolla that she could become her mother if Zezolla killed her stepmother. So Zezolla followed the governess's plan and killed the stepmother.

As Zezolla had hoped, her father married Carmosina. And at first, her new stepmother was kind.

Zezolla

But then the new stepmother revealed a secret—she had six daughters. Poor Zezolla was moved from her room in the palace to the kitchen by the fireplace. They took away her fancy clothes and called her Cenerentola, which means "hearth cat," because like a cat, she spent time near the warm hearth of the fireplace.

One day, the father had to travel to the island of Sardinia. He asked his stepdaughters what they wanted as gifts. They asked for clothes, jewels, makeup, fruits, and flowers. When he asked Zezolla about a gift, she remembered a pigeon that had once landed outside her palace window. It had spoken and told her that if she ever needed anything, she should send a message to the Pigeon of the Fairies in Sardinia. So Zezolla told her father to ask the fairies to give her a gift.

Zezolla's father almost forgot about her, but he did visit the fairies. He came home with a date tree, a mattock (a tool for digging), a bucket, and a napkin they had given him. Zezolla planted the tree in a fine vase. In just a few days, it grew tall. A fairy came out of it and asked her what she wanted.

Zezolla asked to be able to leave the house without her stepsisters knowing. The fairy told her that whenever she wanted to go out, all she had to do was say to the tree:

"My date tree tall and golden,

With a golden mattock I dug thee around
With a golden bucket I watered thee,
With a silken napkin I wiped thee dry:
Undress thyself and robe thou me."

Soon, the king announced a festival. The stepsisters, dressed in their fanciest clothes, headed off for the celebration. Then Zezolla ran to the date tree and said the poem. Suddenly, she was dressed as a queen, with a fine horse and servants to accompany her.

At the festival, the stepsisters were jealous of this beautiful stranger. The king sent his attendant to find out who she was. But Zezolla ran away, throwing coins on the ground to distract him. She made it home in time for the date tree to change her back.

On the second night of the festival, Zezolla went to the tree. This time, girls came out of it with perfume, combs, jewelry, and flowers. They dressed her like a bride. They provided a carriage with horses, footmen, and servants. The king fell even more in love with her. This time, when she realized she was being followed, she tossed jewels and pearls as a distraction.

On the third night of the festival, the tree dressed Zezolla in an even more beautiful gown, and she rode in a golden carriage. This time, she left the festival so quickly that one of her slippers flew out the carriage window. The attendant brought the shoe back to the king.

The king was so in love by then that he invited all women in the land to a banquet. He invited young and old, rich and poor, and he tried the slipper on everyone. But it did not fit any of them. Zezolla's father admitted to the king that he did have another daughter. The king insisted she come to him the next day.

As soon as he saw Zezolla, he knew she was the one. The slipper fit. He told everyone that she was now their queen. The stepsisters, angry and jealous, went home. As with most Cinderella stories, poor Zezolla is treated badly by her wicked stepfamily. Magical helpers come to her rescue. A lost slipper wins her a seat on the throne.

Basile didn't write his story collection for children. Besides writing for entertainment, he also wrote stories to make fun of the different classes in society. *Tale of Tales* is considered the first book of European fairy tales. There were more European Cinderella stories yet to come.

CHAPTER 4
Fairies, Pumpkins, and Glass Shoes

Charles Perrault of France wrote one of the most famous versions of the Cinderella story in 1697. He collected folktales and published them as *Tales of Mother Goose*. Unlike Basile, Perrault wrote his stories specifically for children.

Charles Perrault

In "Cendrillon," or "The Little Glass Slipper," a man had a kind and sweet daughter. He married a woman who was selfish and snobbish, and so were her two daughters. When the new wife took over, she made the girl do all the housework and sleep in a small attic room. The girl dared not even complain to her father. At the end of a tiring day, she rested by the fireplace. The stepmother and stepsisters started calling her Cinderella because she sat among the cinders of the fire.

The prince of the kingdom was hosting a ball,

and the stepsisters talked about nothing except their hairstyles and dresses. They teased Cinderella, but she was kind and helped them prepare. She cried when they left. Her fairy godmother appeared and asked what was wrong. Through her tears, Cinderella admitted that she wanted to go to the ball, too.

Fairy Tales

In the late 1600s, more and more authors gathered oral folktales into written collections. These books were mostly for rich people in the upper classes to read. Many were curious about stories of peasants and other poor folk.

Since then, the term *fairy tale* has come to mean stories with a hero who defeats a villain, and then lives happily ever after. The fairy-tale world often contains magical creatures—like giants, mermaids, witches, and sometimes, but not always, fairies! In fairy tales, characters transform, or change. They often have a lesson for the listener or reader to remember.

Fairy tales often begin with the line "Once upon a time in a faraway land . . ." That's because the stories aren't set in a specific place at a specific time. They could take place anytime and anywhere!

Her fairy godmother told her to fetch a pumpkin from the garden. She struck it with her wand, and it turned into a golden coach! She turned mice into horses, a rat into a coachman, and lizards into footmen. Cinderella still looked sad. The godmother had almost forgotten about a dress! She touched Cinderella with the wand,

and her ragged clothes turned gold and silver. She even gave her glass slippers, the prettiest in the world. As Cinderella climbed into the coach to leave, the fairy godmother warned her not to stay past midnight. If she did, everything would change back to what it had been before.

Word got to the castle that a great princess was arriving! The prince greeted her and led her into the ball. As they danced, everyone saw how graceful she was. No one recognized her as poor

Cinderella. At midnight, she fled. When her sisters arrived home, she pretended she had just woken up. They told her all about the beautiful princess.

The second day of the ball, Cinderella arrived, looking even more beautiful than she had the night before. The prince didn't leave her side. She was having such a wonderful time, she didn't notice the clock was striking midnight. She ran and was already in her old clothes by the time she reached home. All of the things the magic had brought Cinderella were gone, except one glass slipper. The other one had been left behind at the castle when she had hurried away.

A few days later, a trumpet announced that the prince would marry whoever fit the glass slipper. The prince's attendants tried it on the feet of all the princesses, other ladies in the court, and the noblewomen. They came to Cinderella's house. She watched as her two stepsisters tried to force their feet into the slipper. But it would not fit either of them.

"Let me see if it will not fit me," Cinderella said. The stepsisters laughed. Everyone was shocked when her foot slipped right in. Then she took the other slipper out of her pocket to further prove she was the woman the prince was searching for. The fairy godmother appeared, touched her with her wand, and her dress transformed to one even more amazing than before. The stepsisters threw themselves at Cinderella's feet. In her kindness, she forgave them. She was taken to the prince, and they married. She even let her stepsisters live at the palace.

Perrault's story introduces so many parts of the Cinderella fairy tale we know well. He added a fairy godmother, a pumpkin carriage, and a glass slipper. And Perrault also clearly states the moral to be learned. Beauty is a treasure, but kindness is more important. He added another moral, too: It helps to have a godmother to look out for you!

Perrault's version became the basis for many retellings that followed. But there was another version—a scarier version—by the Brothers Grimm.

Charles Perrault (1628–1703)

Charles Perrault was born in Paris, France, into a wealthy family. He studied as a lawyer and then worked for King Louis XIV. He was in charge of the royal buildings and gardens. He was also a writer and a poet, and he often argued that modern writing was better than that of the past.

Perrault is most remembered for his book of fairy tales. Besides "Cinderella," the collection also includes versions of "Little Red Riding-Hood," "Sleeping Beauty," and "Puss in Boots."

Puss in Boots

CHAPTER 5
A Dark Turn

Jacob and Wilhelm Grimm

A little more than one hundred years after Charles Perrault's story collection for children was published in France, in the early 1800s the brothers Jacob and Wilhelm Grimm of Germany also published a collection of tales.

Their book *Children's and Household Tales* included the story "Aschenputtel," which means "ash fool." Tales by the Brothers Grimm are often more violent and scary than other versions. Goodness is rewarded, but villains certainly do not have happy endings!

In "Aschenputtel," a rich man had a wife who was very sick. Before she died, she called her daughter to her bedside and told her an important lesson: *Always be good.*

The man married again to a woman who had two daughters. They were quite beautiful, but the way they treated the man's own daughter was ugly. They laughed at her, took away her dresses, and made her work as a kitchen maid from morning to night. She didn't even have a bed, but instead simply rested by the fireplace. She was always dusty and dirty from the ashes left by the fire, so they called her Aschenputtel.

One day, the father was headed off to a fair, and he asked his stepdaughters what they wanted as gifts. One asked for clothes, the other for jewels. When he asked Aschenputtel the same question, she requested the first branch that struck against his cap on the way home. So that is what he brought her.

Aschenputtel took the twig and planted it on her mother's grave. She cried, and her tears watered the branch. It grew into a tree. She visited it three times a day and cried each time. A white bird rose up from the tree. It told Aschenputtel it could grant her wishes.

The king of the region declared a three-day festival. He wanted all the beautiful young women to come so that the prince, his son, could choose a bride. Aschenputtel wanted to go, but instead, she had to comb her sisters' hair, clean their shoes, and help them get ready. She begged her stepmother to let her go, too. The stepmother tossed a bowlful of lentils into the ashes. She said Aschenputtel could go only if she picked up all the lentils first.

It was an impossible task! But Aschenputtel went out to the garden and called to the birds. White doves, turtle doves, and other birds of all kinds flew inside, pecked at the lentils, and put them all in the bowl. She would go to the festival! But then her stepmother said she could go only if she picked up *two* bowls of lentils from the ashes. Again, Aschenputtel called on the birds for help, and together they refilled the pot.

The stepmother didn't keep her promise. She and her daughters left for the festival. Aschenputtel went out to her wishing tree and asked it to shake its branches and cover her with silver and gold. The tree threw down a dress of gold and silver and a pair of slippers sewn with silk and silver.

Aschenputtel put them on and headed out for the festival.

When Aschenputtel arrived, the stepmother and stepsisters didn't recognize her. They thought she was a princess from another land. The prince refused to dance with anyone else the whole night. When it was late, she wanted to go home. The prince wanted to go with her. So she ran and hid in a pigeon house. She escaped in time to reach home, take off the dress, and sit by the cinders.

The next day of the festival, the tree gave her an even more beautiful dress. This time the prince had been waiting for her. She ran off at the end of the night, and hid in a pear tree. Again, Aschenputtel escaped before she could be found and made it home with no one realizing she had gone.

The third night, she had the grandest dress of all, and this time paired with gold slippers.

At the end of the night, the prince had a plan. He had spread the steps of the palace with sticky tar so that when she rushed away, one of her shoes was left behind. Then the prince declared that he wanted to marry the woman who fit that shoe.

The older stepsister tried on the slipper, but of course it didn't fit. The stepmother pulled her aside and handed her a knife. She told her to cut off a toe. The slipper fit, and the prince mistakenly took the stepsister to be his bride. But as they passed the grave of Aschenputtel's mother, two pigeons in the magical tree told him that the stepsister was not the right woman.

The younger stepsister didn't fit the shoe either, so the stepmother made her cut off her heel. She tricked the prince again, but the pigeons revealed that she was not the bride for the prince either.

Only Aschenputtel was left. She slipped the shoe on her foot. A perfect fit!

The stepsisters came to the wedding. But as punishment, the pigeons pecked out their eyes for being so wicked.

This version from the Grimm Brothers is one of the most violent. The selfish characters are severely punished for their wickedness. This

Cinderella story doesn't have a fairy godmother. Instead, the tree, with the spirit of her mother, provides Aschenputtel with what she needs. Her goodness, though, is what really grants her all her wishes. And like Perrault's Cinderella, the Grimm Brothers' tale takes a plot we have seen in stories before it and transforms it into something new.

Jacob Grimm (1785–1863) and Wilhelm Grimm (1786–1859)

The Grimm Brothers grew up in the small German town of Kassel. After both of their parents died, Jacob, the oldest, was in charge of Wilhelm and his other three brothers and a sister. The two young men liked to study, and they were the perfect pair to create one of the most famous collections of fairy tales in history.

After studying law and language, the brothers became interested in folktales. They spent their time working in libraries and collecting tales from friends, relatives, and others. They looked for oral stories that had been told for centuries, but never written down. The brothers collected them so they would be remembered.

Children's and Household Tales, which included more than 150 stories, was published in two volumes between 1812 and 1815. Besides "Aschenputtel," it also included the familiar "Snow White," "Hansel and Gretel," "Rapunzel," and "Sleeping Beauty."

Rapunzel

CHAPTER 6
Stepping Off the Page

Throughout the 1800s, Cinderella wasn't found just in books. She became a character onstage. In 1813, the Austrian ballet master Louis Antoine Duport first transformed Perrault's version of the Cinderella story into a ballet. Then in 1817, Gioachino Rossini of Italy wrote an opera. On a stage in Rome, Italy, audiences met stepfather Don Magnifico, his stepdaughter and the title character Cenerentola, and Prince Ramiro. But magic doesn't bring the couple together in this version. Instead, Cenerentola falls in love with the prince when he is disguised as a servant.

In the early 1900s, movies became a new way to tell stories, too. Directors looked for subjects that they knew audiences would enjoy. So it is no surprise that Cinderella appeared on movie screens. At first, movies were filmed in black and white with no sound. In 1914, a silent movie *Cinderella* was released. It starred the popular actress Mary Pickford, who people called the Queen of the Movies.

Mary Pickford as Cinderella

An animator named Walt Disney was also becoming a big name in the movies. In 1922, he made a seven-minute black-and-white version of the Cinderella story. Cinderella, the prince, and all the usual characters appear, along with lots of silly cartoon animals.

A few decades later, he decided to make a full-length movie about Cinderella. He filmed live actors first. Then his animators used that film as a model to draw the pictures. Musicians composed songs, and Ilene Woods sang and voiced Cinderella. To celebrate the movie, Disney Studios held a glittery "Cinderella Ball" in New York City, where Ilene Woods was crowned queen. Fans of all ages were eager to see *Cinderella* when it opened on February 15, 1950. Hundreds of people lined up outside the Mayfair Theatre for tickets.

Disney based his version of the Cinderella story on Perrault's tale. As in Perrault's story, the stepmother is cruel and the stepsisters are selfish. Cinderella is forced to be a servant in her own house. Even so, she is gentle and kind, and she always looks for the goodness in others. Forced to live in an attic room, she dreams of a better life. Disney's version adds lots of animals. Birds and mice keep Cinderella company and sing with her about her dreams.

The king invites all the maidens in the kingdom to a ball to find a wife for his son Prince Charming. The stepmother says Cinderella can go, but only if she can get all her work done and find something suitable to wear. While Cinderella works hard all day, the mice and birds sew her a dress. But when her stepmother and stepsisters see it, they rip the dress to shreds and leave her behind.

Cinderella runs to the garden. "It's just no use. No use at all . . . ," she cries. "There's nothing left to believe in." Cinderella's sadness draws the attention of the fairy godmother, who makes her dreams come true. With her magic wand, and her song "Bibbidi-Bobbodi-Boo," she turns a pumpkin into a coach, and animals into horses and attendants. Cinderella's ripped dress becomes a beautiful silver-blue gown, and glass slippers shimmer on her feet. And just as in Perrault's version of the story, she's warned that the magic will last only until midnight.

As with other versions of the fairy tale, the prince falls in love at first sight and dances with Cinderella. She rushes away at midnight, leaving a slipper behind. All the women of the kingdom try it on. But in Disney's version of the story, the animals come to the rescue. The stepmother has locked Cinderella in the attic, and the mice steal the key to get her out. They are chased by Lucifer the cat, the birds fight back, and Bruno the dog finally scares the cat away. The animals save the day. And the movie ends with wedding bells!

Walt Disney's *Cinderella* was a huge hit. And it has become a classic. Even though it came out more than seventy years ago, people still know many of the songs by heart. Lots of the details that people think of when they think of Cinderella—such as her blue dress, mice helpers, and familiar songs—were created by Disney. And you can even visit her castle at the Magic Kingdom in Walt Disney World in Florida.

Walt Disney (1901–1966)

Walt Disney was born in Chicago, Illinois, and started his creative career as an artist for his high school newspaper. When he discovered animation, he started a company in Kansas City, Missouri, called Laugh-o-grams and made short cartoons. In 1923, he went to Hollywood to become a director and started an animation studio with his brother Roy. By 1928, he had created Mickey Mouse, one of his most famous characters.

Disney Studios produced lots of cartoon shorts. In 1937, Disney proved that audiences were willing to watch full-length animated movies, too. *Snow White and the Seven Dwarfs* amazed and delighted audiences with its memorable characters and music. Along with lots of other stories, Disney continued to produce even more movies about princesses, including Cinderella, Ariel, Rapunzel, Aurora, Belle, Tiana, Mulan, Jasmine, and Pocahontas.

CHAPTER 7
A Popular Princess

Also in the 1950s, two award-winning writers got together to write a Cinderella story. Richard Rodgers was a music composer, and Oscar Hammerstein wrote lyrics. They had worked on musical shows for the Broadway stage. But this show would be for television. *Rodgers and Hammerstein's Cinderella*, starring Julie Andrews, was filmed live and aired on March 31, 1957. Since it was viewed on television instead of in a theater, it reached a big audience. More than one hundred million people watched it!

Like Disney's movie, *Rodgers and Hammerstein's Cinderella* stuck close to Perrault's story and added memorable songs, including "The Prince Is Giving a Ball." The king and queen are throwing a party for their son, Prince Christopher, to find him a wife. Meanwhile, Cinderella is being bossed around by her stepmother and stepsisters. She sings "In My Own Little Corner," a song about the one spot in her house, near the fireplace, where she can be whatever she wants to be.

When her fairy godmother appears, she tells Cinderella that wishing isn't enough. She has to help herself. She sings the song "Impossible" about how it is impossible for a pumpkin to become a carriage and for mice to be horses. But it is also true that impossible things happen every day. And of course, they happen for Cinderella!

As in other versions of the story, Cinderella

and the prince fall in love at the ball, and she runs away. The prince has all the maidens of the kingdom try on the shoe she left behind. But in this show, Cinderella is not even home when the prince visits her house. Instead, she's hiding in the palace garden. She's afraid that he won't love her if he knows she's a servant. The guards find her, she tries on the shoe—it fits!

Rodgers and Hammerstein's Cinderella aired on television again in 1965 with new actors, including teenager Lesley Ann Warren, who went on to become quite famous. One of the most popular television versions of *Rodgers and Hammerstein's Cinderella* was broadcast in 1997 with a star-studded cast. Brandy Norwood became the first Black actress to play Cinderella.

Brandy Norwood

Whitney Houston, the famous singer, played her fairy godmother. The cast also included the actors Whoopi Goldberg as Queen Constantina and Paolo Montalban as Prince Christopher. Like earlier versions, it shared an important theme: Sometimes impossible things can be possible. By the end, Cinderella has left her own little corner and can be whatever she wants to be.

Rodgers and Hammerstein's version was also performed on Broadway from 2013 to 2015 and was nominated for nine Tony Awards, which are given for excellence in American theater. Audiences watched Cinderella's dress seem to magically transform onstage. But it wasn't magic. The costume was so amazing that the designer William Ivey Long won the Tony Award for Best Costume Design of a Musical.

Richard Rodgers (1902–1979) and Oscar Hammerstein II (1895–1960)

Rodgers was a composer, a musician who writes the music. Hammerstein was a lyricist, a musician who writes the lyrics, or words, to songs.

Rodgers started writing musical comedies while

in college and then worked hard at a successful composing career. He wrote scores for shows that played on Broadway in New York City, the West End in London, England, and then Hollywood, California. Hammerstein also started writing musical comedies in college. He went on to write lyrics to many more shows.

Rodgers and Hammerstein had met when they were young men, and even wrote some music together back then. In 1943, the two men were reunited and collaborated on *Oklahoma!*, a musical about a farm girl and a cowboy who fall in love. It ran on Broadway for more than two thousand performances. From then on, Rodgers and Hammerstein became one of the most famous musical partnerships in Broadway history. Some of the other famous shows they wrote for the stage include *Carousel*, *South Pacific*, *The King and I*, and *The Sound of Music*. They also wrote *State*

Fair, a movie musical, and *Cinderella*, a musical produced live for television. They won dozens of awards.

Rodgers continued to write musicals even after Hammerstein died, and the Richard Rodgers Theatre on Broadway is named for him.

Cinderella stories are performed onstage, shown on television, and published as books and collections all over the world. Writers have even combined fairy tales within a single production, like in the musical *Into the Woods* on Broadway, which includes references to "Cinderella," "Little Red Riding Hood," and "Jack and the Beanstalk." The television show *Once Upon a Time* is set in a town filled with cursed fairy-tale characters. And in *Shrek the Third*, Cinderella, along with Snow White, Sleeping Beauty, and Rapunzel join forces with Princess Fiona to try to rescue Shrek.

But people weren't done telling Cinderella's story. She still had more balls to attend, shoes to lose, and kingdoms to rule.

A Cinderella Story

Cinderella is so popular, that she is even a part of our language. The term *a Cinderella story* describes anyone who is not expected to be successful. Perhaps they are poor or are treated unfairly. By the end, they achieve great things and their dreams come true. The term is often used in sports when a team unlikely to win ends up winning the whole championship!

One of the most famous Cinderella stories in sports history has become known as the Miracle on Ice. At the 1980 Winter Olympics, in Lake Placid, New York, the US men's hockey team played against the Soviet Union team. No one expected the United States to win. After all, the Soviets had won the gold medal at the previous four Winter Olympics. And when the United States and Soviets played each other, the Soviets often won.

But the coach of the US team, Herb Brooks, worked the players hard, and they practiced a lot. The game was close, but Team USA beat the Soviets 4–3. They went on to play Finland, win that game, and take home the gold.

CHAPTER 8
Her Own Hero

By the late 1900s, writers started thinking of Cinderella in a new way. What if she didn't need to be saved from her hard life by a prince? What if she could save herself?

The 1998 movie *Ever After: A Cinderella Story* created a whole new Cinderella. It was inspired by Charles Perrault's story and set in sixteenth-century France. The story has many of the familiar fictional characters, including the stepmother, stepsisters, and a prince. But it also includes characters based on historical figures such as Leonardo da Vinci and the Grimm Brothers.

The movie begins with a royal woman telling the Brothers Grimm that they got their fairy tale wrong. She goes on to tell the "true" story of Danielle, a smart and independent girl, who is forced to work as a servant for her stepmother.

Leonardo da Vinci

Danielle's dress

Danielle, who is played by actress Drew Barrymore, has strong opinions about fairness for peasants in the kingdom. Dressed as a noble, she meets Prince Henry. He is curious about her ideas. She is unlike the other women he's met. They fall in love. Once, on a walk in the woods, she even saves him from a band of thieves!

Danielle's stepmother finds out what she is up

to and locks her up on the night of the grand ball hosted by Prince Henry that Danielle wanted to attend. Leonardo, a fairy-godmother-like character, gets her to the ball. But the stepmother reveals to the prince that Danielle has been lying. She is not a noblewoman. She is just a servant.

The stepmother sells Danielle off to someone else to marry. She is trapped. The prince runs after her to save her, but she's already pulled a sword on her captor and has saved herself before he even gets there. They marry, she becomes queen, and the stepmother ends up working for her in the palace laundry. *Ever After* is another version of the story that shows being unkind comes with consequences!

Danielle

The woman telling the story to the Grimm Brothers reveals that she is the great great-granddaughter of Danielle, and she has the shoe to prove it. This Cinderella doesn't need magic. She uses her own passion and strength to save herself. There is no fairy godmother or magical white bird in this story—just a determined young woman.

Ella of Frell is another Cinderella character who

stands up for herself and others in the kingdom. *Ella Enchanted* is a popular book published by author Gail Carson Levine in 1997. In 2004 it was made into a movie of the same title starring Anne Hathaway. While it is set in the past like many other versions of the story, it is silly and funny with modern songs and details. When Ella is born, a fairy godmother gives her the gift of obedience. Ella must always do what she's told. As she grows older, this becomes a big problem. Especially when her stepsister discovers her secret. Obedience is not a gift—it's a curse.

Meanwhile, all the maidens of the kingdom are in love with Prince Char. He's soon to be king, and Ella hopes he'll change some of the rules of the kingdom, where ogres, giants, and elves are treated unfairly. When Char flees from his screaming fans, he runs into Ella. He likes her ideas for a fairer kingdom, and they fall in love.

Ogre

Char's uncle wants to be king and discovers Ella's curse of obedience. He orders her to kill Char, and she must obey his command. She tries to stay away from him, but it's impossible. As she's about to kill Char, she remembers what her mother said before she died: "What's inside you is stronger than any spell." She's able to break the curse.

The uncle locks her up and plans to kill Char himself with a poisoned crown. The ogres, giants, and elves come to their rescue. Char and Ella marry, and they rule over a kingdom where everyone is equal. This new type of Cinderella still falls in love with the prince and rules the kingdom with him at the end. But she uses her own smarts, courage, and kindness to get herself there.

CHAPTER 9
A Modern Cinderella

Cinderella stories are often set in the past or a faraway land in a fairy-tale kingdom. In 2004, however, the movie *A Cinderella Story* with actress Hilary Duff set the familiar tale in an American high school. Sam, a teenager, lives in California with her father, who owns a diner. They play baseball together, and he reads her fairy tales. He has a favorite saying: *Never let the fear of striking out keep you from playing the game.* He marries Fiona, who has twin daughters Sam's age. But he

Hilary Duff

dies, and Sam's new family is cruel to her. Fiona makes Sam work at the diner, while she sits by the pool with her daughters.

Meanwhile, the popular kids in school, including football star Austin, are like royalty. Sam and Austin become friends over texts and emails. But he doesn't know that she's just "diner girl." During the Halloween dance at school, they dance, but he still doesn't know it's Sam because she is wearing a costume with a mask. She drops her cell phone on the way out. The phone is locked, and Austin can't figure out who it belongs to.

Sam is afraid to tell Austin who she really is, but then she remembers her dad's saying. She doesn't let fear hold her back. She tells him the truth, stands up to her stepmother, and quits her job. She also finds out that she actually owns the diner. So in the end, the stepmother and stepsisters are working for her!

Some newer Cinderella stories are still set in the past, including Disney's 2015 live-action *Cinderella* with Lily James. This one doesn't have ogres or talking mice, but it does have plenty of magic, with its pumpkin carriage, animal attendants, and glass slippers. The most important message comes as advice from Cinderella's mother before she dies: "Have courage and be kind." Her courage and kindness, not her fancy dress or shoes, are what win Cinderella her royal position in the end.

Lily James

Another Cinderella movie set in fairy-tale times stars the singer Camila Cabello. In this 2021 version simply called *Cinderella*, Ella's dream is to open her own dress shop, but everyone tells her that women can't run businesses. She's the kind of girl who breaks the rules. She sells a dress at the market, not knowing the buyer is Prince Robert in disguise. He tells her she should go to the ball to get her dress designs noticed.

She creates a beautiful dress of her own design, but her unkind stepmother destroys it and tells her she can't go to the ball. Sad in the garden, Ella meets her Fabulous Godmother, or "Fab G." He brings one of Ella's dress designs to life—a new one that Ella didn't think was even possible to make—and everyone at the ball notices it. She dances with the prince, who picks her to be his princess. But she doesn't want to give up her work. She wants to follow her dream.

After she runs away at midnight and leaves a slipper behind, she realizes she loves Prince Robert. And he says he is willing to give up the kingdom for her. They decide to travel the world together as she takes a job as personal dressmaker to the queen of a different kingdom. The moral of this story is that no one can tell you what you should do with your life. You can do it your way.

One of the most recent Cinderella-inspired movies is not about a young girl from the countryside. It's about a boy who lives in the city. The 2022 film *Sneakerella* introduces El, a kind and creative boy who lives in Queens, a borough of New York City. He dreams of designing sneakers, but his stepfather makes him work as a stock boy in the family shoe store. His selfish stepbrothers tease him and don't have to work hard like he does.

He meets a girl named Kira, not knowing that she is the daughter of Darius King, the owner of a major sneaker company. When El realizes she's "sneaker royalty," he decides to design a new sneaker and go to a gala to see Kira again. The night of the big event, his stepbrothers lock him in the stockroom at the shoe store. Gustavo, the community gardener, lets him out. And with what seems like a little magic, Gustavo provides him with an orange convertible and tickets to get into the gala. Everyone notices his shoes and thinks El is a hot new designer. But when he runs off before midnight, his sneaker gets caught in the escalator, and he has to leave it behind.

Kira uses social media to find him and sets up a meeting with El and her father. But the stepbrothers mess it up for El by telling Kira's father the truth—he's not really a designer. El gives up, tossing all his designs in the trash. But Gustavo and the magic of the neighborhood turn one of his designs into real sneakers. The next day,

El takes them to Kira as a gift. He had been afraid to tell her that he was just a stock boy. By the end of the movie, he becomes a sneaker designer for Darius King's company. The moral? If you believe in yourself, anything is possible.

Cinderella, and her story, have been growing and changing for thousands of years. Very few characters have lived that long! The prince's name may change. Even Cinderella's name changes sometimes! And the shoe has been made of silk, gold, and glass. Sometimes it's a sandal, and sometimes it's a sneaker. But Cinderella's goodness has not changed through the years. It is the most important part of most Cinderella stories.

Cinderella's story has been told and retold over time because we all have dreams, and we all have challenges to overcome. Sometimes they are big and sometimes they are small. We might not see ourselves at a ball or marrying a prince, but everyone has unique and special hopes for the future.

Even though her story has changed over the years, the character of Cinderella has always represented a hardworking and hopeful person who believes in the possibilities of transformation.

Life might seem unfair, or even cruel. But kindness and courage can overcome hardship. And dreams really do come true.

Bibliography

Branagh, Kenneth, director. *Cinderella*. Walt Disney Studios, 2015. DVD.

Cannon, Kay, director. *Cinderella*. Amazon Studios, 2021. Amazon Prime Video.

Dubin, Charles S., director. ***Rodgers and Hammerstein's Cinderella***. CBS, 1965. DVD.

Gabler, Neal. ***Walt Disney: The Triumph of the American Imagination***. New York: Alfred A. Knopf, 2006.

Geronimi, Clyde, Wilfred Jackson, and Hamilton Luske, directors. ***Cinderella***. Disney Studios, 1950. Disney+.

Griffith, John W., and Charles H. Frey, editor. ***Classics of Children's Literature***, 3rd edition. New York: Macmillan Publishing Company, 1992.

Iscove, Robert, director. ***Rodgers and Hammerstein's Cinderella***. Walt Disney Television, 1997. Disney+.

Jubber, Nicholas. ***The Fairy Tellers: A Journey into the Secret History of Fairy Tales***. Boston: Nicholas Brealey Publishing, 2022.

"Keke Palmer to Be First African American 'Cinderella' on Broadway." **ABC News**. September 9, 2014. YouTube video, 4:24. https://www.youtube.com/watch?v=SasefDllN-U.

Lang, Andrew, editor. ***Perrault's Popular Tales***. New York: Arno Press, 1977.

Miller, Julie. "Keke Palmer on Becoming Broadway's First African-American Cinderella." *Vanity Fair*, August 4, 2014. https://www.vanityfair.com/hollywood/2014/08/keke-palmer-cinderella-broadway.

Nelson, Ralph, director. *Rodgers and Hammerstein's Cinderella*. CBS, 1957. YouTube. https://www.youtube.com/watch?v=C1F4YhBOA14.

O'Haver, Tommy, director. *Ella Enchanted*. Miramax, 2004. DVD.

Paradiz, Valerie. *Clever Maids: The Secret History of the Grimm Fairy Tales*. New York: Basic Books, 2005.

Perrault, Charles. *Charles Perrault: Memoirs of My Life*. Translated by Jeanne Morgan Zarucchi. Columbia, Missouri: University of Missouri Press, 1989.

Rosenbaum, Elizabeth Allen, director. *Sneakerella*. Disney+, 2022.

Rosman, Mark, director. *A Cinderella Story*. Warner Bros., 2004. DVD.

Seastrom, Lucas. "The History, Debut, and Impact of Disney's Classic *Cinderella*." **The Walt Disney Family Museum Blog**. August 3, 2020. https://www.waltdisney.org/blog/history-debut-and-impact-disneys-classic-cinderella.

Tatar, Maria, editor. *The Classic Fairy Tales*. New York: W.W. Norton & Company, 2017.

Tennant, Andy, director. ***Ever After: A Cinderella Story***. 20th Century Studios, 1998. DVD.

Thayer, Bill. "The Geography of Strabo." Loeb Classical Library edition, 1932. https://penelope.uchicago.edu/Thayer/e/roman/texts/strabo/17a3*.html.

Waley, Arthur. "The Chinese Cinderella Story." ***Folklore***, March 1947, Vol. 58, No. 1, pp. 226–238.

Zipes, Jack. ***When Dreams Came True: Classical Fairy Tales and Their Tradition***. Oxfordshire, England: Routledge, 1999.

Website

rodgersandhammerstein.com/show/cinderella